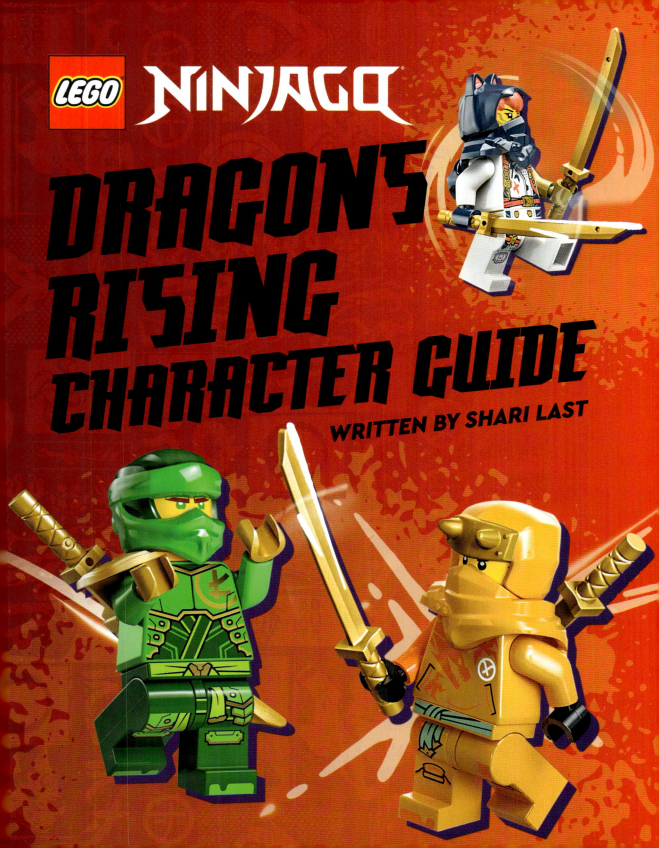

CONTENTS

4 WELCOME TO NINJAGO!

HEROES
8 ARIN
9 SORA
10 MASTER WU
11 LLOYD
12 KAI
13 WYLDFYRE
14 DESTINY'S BOUNTY
16 CITY MARKETS
18 CROSSROADS CITIZENS
20 HEROES IN BATTLE
22 NYA
23 JAY
24 ZANE
25 COLE
26 TEMPLE OF THE DRAGON ENERGY CORES
28 NINJA POWER

VILLAINS

- 32 EMPRESS BEATRIX
- 33 LORD RAS
- 34 IMPERIUM GUARD
- 35 IMPERIUM GUARD COMMANDER
- 36 DRAGON HUNTER HOUND
- 38 IMPERIUM CLAW HUNTER
- 39 IMPERIUM CLAW GENERAL
- 40 RAPTON
- 41 JORDANA
- 42 CINDER
- 43 WOLF MASK WARRIOR
- 44 WOLF MASK SHADOW DOJO

DRAGONS

- 48 SOURCE DRAGON
- 50 EGALT
- 52 HEATWAVE
- 54 JIRO
- 56 RIYU
- 57 RISING DRAGON
- 58 DRAGON STONE SHRINE

- 60 GLOSSARY
- 62 INDEX

WELCOME TO NINJAGO!

In Ninjago a battle is raging—over dragons! Empress Beatrix, ruler of Imperium, commands her Claw Hunter army to capture dragons and drain them of their power. Meanwhile, the fearsome warrior Lord Ras is hiding cruel plans of his own. But watch out, villains! The Ninja and their new team of amazing friends are ready to fight the forces of evil.

Discover the heroes and villains who are preparing for battle, and get a close-up look at their awesome weapons, vehicles, mechs, and more. So let's go and join the Ninja on their quest to save all dragons!

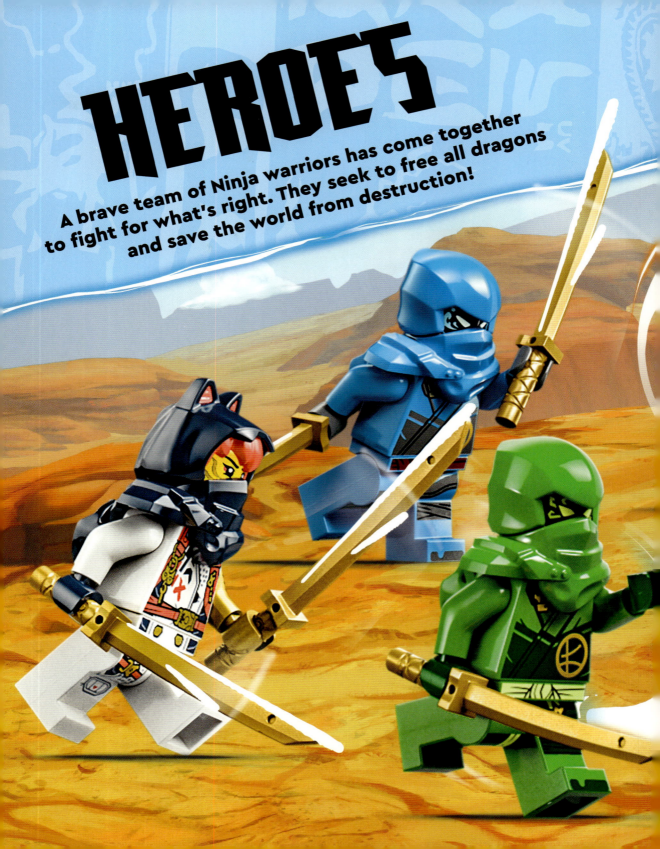

ARIN WANNABE NINJA

Arin is a Ninja superfan who taught himself a rough form of the martial arts technique, Spinjitzu. Along with his best friend Sora, Arin does his best to keep the Crossroads safe. His wish is to have a real Ninja Master teach him how to be a hero.

Ninja robes are the same style as Arin's old sweater

Handy pockets for snacks

FACT FILE

Known for: Being helpful but clumsy
Likes: Anything to do with Ninja
Dislikes: Mud soup
Watch out for: His delicious snowberry pies

WOW!
Arin has the unique ability to transfer Spinjitzu energy to other objects. That's a useful skill when battling baddies!

NINJA IN TRAINING
Arin couldn't believe his eyes when he met Lloyd, the Green Ninja, in real life! His dreams of becoming a Ninja came true when he began his training.

SORA MASTER OF TECHNOLOGY

Tech whiz Sora met Arin and a baby dragon named Riyu in the Crossroads. She soon realized that Riyu somehow activates her Elemental Powers! Sora doesn't always trust in her own skills, but her inventions get the Ninja out of all kinds of trouble.

Cat-ear hood

TECH GENIUS
Sora can reprogram machines at lightning speed. That's pretty handy if you want robot enemies to stop chasing you and dance instead!

FACT FILE
Known for: Cat-themed clothing style
Likes: Candied mushrooms
Dislikes: Early morning training
Watch out for: Her genius at transforming vehicles

WOW!
Sora grew up in Imperium, but ran away after scientist Dr. LaRow tried to use her inventions to harm dragons.

MASTER WU
MISSING MASTER OF CREATION

Wu disappeared after the Merge—an event where all known Realms joined together as one land. However, the Ninja have a funny feeling their former Master is still guiding them...

Signature conical hat

Traditional sensei robes

FACT FILE
Known for: Wise advice
Likes: Teaching in mysterious ways
Dislikes: Cold tea
Watch out for: His mischievous streak!

Ornate gold hem details

WOW!
Wu astonishes the Ninja with his knowledge of Ninjago's history and secrets. If only he was around to help them learn about the Merge!

SPECTRAL WISDOM
Wu appears to Lloyd when the Green Ninja needs him most. Emerging as a golden vision, he often helps Lloyd find calm in the heat of a battle.

LLOYD MASTER OF ENERGY

Brave Lloyd has saved Ninjago many times with his former team, but now he must rise to new challenges. Training the next generation of heroes and saving the United Realms is no easy task!

Eyes reveal Green Ninja Energy

Letter "L" symbol

FACT FILE
Known for: Leading Team Ninja
Likes: Encouraging others
Dislikes: Master Wu's carpet getting messy!
Watch out for: Unique training methods

DRAGON ENERGY
Lloyd searched for a set of three Dragon Energy Cores. These held the power to stabilize the MergeQuakes and save Ninjago.

WOW!
Despite being the legendary Green Ninja, Lloyd sometimes struggles to keep his Ninja pupils in check. Master Wu always made it look so easy!

KAI MASTER OF FIRE

Kai traveled to faraway Realms, trying to discover what was causing the dangerous MergeQuakes—the aftershocks of the Merge. When he returned, he met a new Elemental Master with fire powers.

Gold buckles secure robes during battle

Letter "K" symbol

FACT FILE
Known for: Bringing humor to battle
Likes: The "Kai" hairstyle
Dislikes: Fireproof monsters
Watch out for: His fiery dragon race car

WOW!
Kai was traveling through the Realms on Team Ninja's old ship, the Destiny's Bounty.

UNDERGROUND JOURNEY
Kai made an amazing discovery thanks to a strange golden light. It guided him to a curious gate far below the Monastery of Spinjitzu.

WYLDFYRE MASTER OF HEAT

Wyldfyre is as wild and fiery as her name suggests! Meeting the Ninja gave her a whole new perspective on life—she realized she could learn a lot from her new Ninja friends.

POWERS UNITE

Kai saw Wyldfyre as a rival when he discovered she had fire powers. But the pair unites on their mission to protect the dragons of Imperium.

- Horned headpiece tied in hair
- Belt buckle is a bone from the Wyldness

FACT FILE

Known for: *Raw fire powers*
Likes: *Fresh fruit*
Dislikes: *Being told something is too dangerous*
Watch out for: *Her loyal dragon friend, Heatwave*

WOW!

Wyldfyre had an unusual childhood. She was raised in the Wyldness by a robot nanny and a fire-breathing dragon!

DESTINY'S BOUNTY

Traveling with the Ninja got a whole lot cooler after Sora fixed up the newer, sleeker Destiny's Bounty. Hurtling through the skies, this awesome airship can swiftly dodge the Ninja's enemies. See ya later, villains!

SORA'S CHALLENGE
Exploring the United Realms, the Ninja visit many unusual locations. Use your bricks to create a wild new place to discover!

Adjustable sails

Handrail with dragon-head ends

Table set for a Ninja tea break

WOW!
When Arin and Lloyd crashed the Bounty into the sea, they had to fight off a monstrous crab before they could repair the ship!

Anchor can be used to lower the Ninja to the ground

SET NAME: Destiny's Bounty—Race Against Time
SET NUMBER: 71797
PIECES: 1,739
MINIFIGURES: 6

POST-MERGE

The old Bounty was the Ninja's trusty ship for years. It survived the Merge, but was later destroyed by Earth Dragons.

Living quarters

Rotating engines help the Bounty change direction

BATTLE BUDDIES

When they're not busy battling their enemies, the Ninja fight fiercely against each other—but only on the playroom games machine, of course!

15

CITY MARKETS

The Merge ripped through every Realm at once. At its center a new neighborhood formed, known as the Crossroads. Here, people from different Realms clash and connect in a noisy, thriving community—many of them living and playing in the vibrant City Markets.

The Borg Store

Fresh produce for sale at the floating market

LOCAL HANGOUT

The Ninja were pleased to spot their old friend Dareth at a cool bar in the Crossroads. When they're not on Ninja duty, the team likes to hang out here playing darts and pool.

SET NAME: NINJAGO® City Markets
SET NUMBER: 71799
PIECES: 6,163
MINIFIGURES: 21

WOW!
The Crossroads Cable Car offers views of the busy city below. From it you can see the red bridge—a rare place of calm amid the bustle.

SORA'S CHALLENGE
The Crossroads has a mix of cultures from every Realm—and it works! Get together with your friends and build something new using everyone's craziest ideas!

CROSSROADS CARNIVAL
The annual Crossroads Carnival is often a night to remember. Visitors won't want to miss the skull juggling, pie contests, snow cones, and the incredible fireworks display!

Cameraman Vinny Folson records Gayle Gossip's broadcast

CROSSROADS CITIZENS

Waking up in a strange place with people from other Realms was a shock. But the citizens of the Crossroads learned to make the most of their new home. Most of them love living in such a vibrant city.

Stars decorate armored vest

CHAMILLE
This Elemental Master of Form last saw the Ninja at the Tournament of Elements, ages ago. She has no idea how she ended up in the Crossroads, but she's building a reputation as a top hairdresser.

Sheriff badge never removed

HOUNDDOG MCBRAG
He used to be the toughest sheriff in Ninjago, but Hounddog McBrag doesn't have an official sheriff title in the Crossroads. That doesn't stop him from trying to enforce law and order, though!

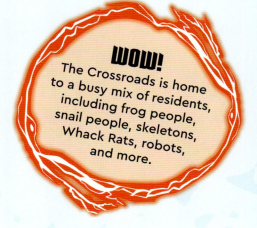

WOW! The Crossroads is home to a busy mix of residents, including frog people, snail people, skeletons, Whack Rats, robots, and more.

Shirt shows Blazey is a fan of BIONICLE® construction toys

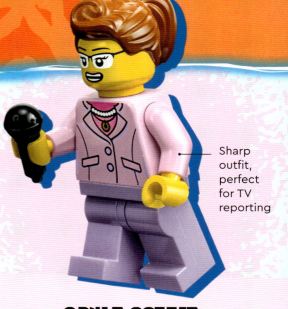

Sharp outfit, perfect for TV reporting

GAYLE GOSSIP

NGTV's top news reporter was shocked by the Merge, but she didn't skip a beat. Gayle continues to report from the Crossroads, on everything from Dragon Hunter attacks to tea shortages!

BLAZEY H. SPEED

Known as Racer 7 in the video game *Prime Empire*, Blazey changed her name when she moved to Ninjago. Now a citizen of the Crossroads, she loves tasting food from all the different Realms.

Cybernetic hand

CYRUS BORG

No longer corrupted by the Overlord, genius inventor Cyrus Borg loves his new life in the Crossroads. He works in his lab above the Borg Store, coming up with amazing new technology.

HEROES IN BATTLE

Fighting Empress Beatrix and her Claw Hunter army was no easy task. But true heroes always find a way to rise to the challenge. Team Ninja stands tall in their incredible high-tech mechs, which range from transforming speedsters to sleek training machines.

SET NAME: Sora's Transforming Mech Bike Racer
SET NUMBER: 71792
PIECES: 384
MINIFIGURES: 3

Mech arms can hold weapons

Arin's mech docks onto Lloyd's

Legs move back to transform into bike

MECH BIKE RACER
Even in the middle of a race, Sora is always ready to launch into battle! Using her Elemental Tech Powers, Sora can transform her racing bike into a powerful mech.

NINJA TEAM MECHS

This large green mech and the smaller yellow mech combine into one fearsome battle machine. Lloyd and Arin discover that to work this formidable mech it takes top teamwork!

ELEMENTAL FIRE MECH

Kai towers over his enemies in his mech. Its sturdy armored body protects Kai as he pilots from its chest cockpit. The huge golden blade harnesses Kai's fire powers.

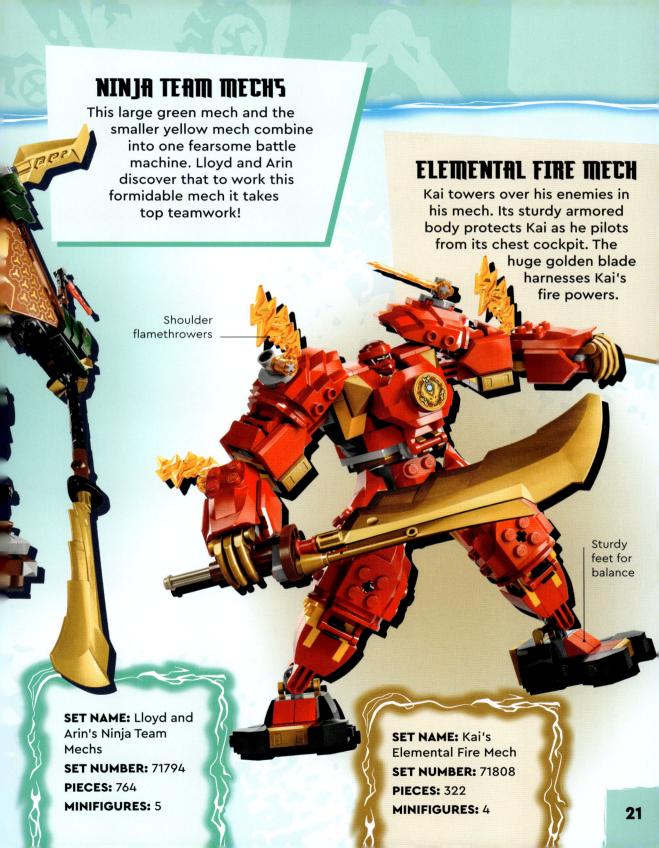

Shoulder flamethrowers

Sturdy feet for balance

SET NAME: Lloyd and Arin's Ninja Team Mechs
SET NUMBER: 71794
PIECES: 764
MINIFIGURES: 5

SET NAME: Kai's Elemental Fire Mech
SET NUMBER: 71808
PIECES: 322
MINIFIGURES: 4

NYA MASTER OF WATER

Practical and determined, Nya has spent the last year trying to find out all she can about the mysterious Merge. She's impressed with Sora's tech skills and wants to help the young Elemental Master find her power within.

BATTLE PLAN
Nya's smart moves and even smarter ideas helped defend Cloud Kingdom from a tentacled monster. Nya blasted water at the creature, forcing it back into its own Realm.

Flexible armored skirt allows for movement in battle

Toe guards essential for Ninja kicks

WOW!
After the Merge, Nya lived for a while with the Craglings in the Kingdom of Madness. Their king called her "Ninja Nya."

FACT FILE
Known for: Inventive ideas

Likes: Libraries and archives

Dislikes: Not having a plan

Watch out for: Powerful bursts of water energy

JAY MASTER OF LIGHTNING

Once the fast-talking Ninja of Lightning, Jay has been known as Agent Walker since the Merge. He doesn't seem to remember anything about his past and is now shockingly serious!

FACT FILE
Known for: His snappy suit
Likes: Video games
Dislikes: Standing in line
Watch out for: His detailed knowledge of the Administration building

Armored shoulder guard

Yellow sash tied in a traditional knot

ALL WORK AND SOME PLAY
Agent Walker works for the Administration. His job appears to be super-serious, but he still plays a few sneaky video games when no one's watching!

WOW!
The Administration has a Teleportation Room. But you'll have to line up for ages to get in there!

ZANE MASTER OF ICE

- Metal Nindroid face
- Ice shard pattern
- Robes the color of ice

Zane went offline after the Merge, but Nya and Kai found him in a newly discovered underground Monastery. Once activated, Zane joined the Ninja in their fight against Imperium.

IMMENSE DISCOVERY

Zane sensed an enormous power source below Imperium. When he and Lloyd investigated, they found themselves face to face with the largest dragon they'd ever seen!

WOW!

As a Nindroid, Zane's brain is a computer. He can analyze data with ease, and even link his mind to machines.

FACT FILE

Known for: *A serious personality*
Likes: *Numbers*
Dislikes: *Chaos*
Watch out for: *His dragon-powered spinning car*

COLE MASTER OF EARTH

Even while living in the Land of Lost Things, Cole never lost his desire to help people! He protected a group of teenagers from a scary monster, and when he reunited with the Ninja he was ready to help them, too.

FACT FILE
Known for: Leadership skills
Likes: His new friends, the Finders
Dislikes: Scavenging
Watch out for: His powerful punch

Buckles with dragon-scale pattern

Wraps protect knees

THE ROOKERY
Cole's home in the Land of Lost Things is known as the Rookery. Inside, there's a strange machine that helps keep the Hoarder monster away.

WOW!
Since the Merge, Cole has a new power. He can cover his entire body in stone armor. This turns him into a fearsome creature!

TEMPLE OF THE DRAGON ENERGY CORES

Team Ninja discovered a mysterious temple inside an ancient tree at the heart of the World Forest. It was full of old statues, strange ornaments, and difficult riddles. The race was on to solve the clues before Empress Beatrix's troops arrived!

CORE HUNT
Unlocking the secrets of the temple will reveal the location of three powerful Dragon Cores. Lloyd was able to request their locations from the wise Spirit of the Temple.

SORA'S CHALLENGE
The temple is protected by many hidden traps. Do you have any hinged or flexible LEGO® elements you could use to create your own defensive traps? Be sneaky!

Ancient well

NINJA POWER

Elemental Powers are what give the Ninja their edge, but when they jump into their supercharged vehicles, they can certainly count on an extra boost!

OFF-ROAD BUGGY

The bumpy dirt roads of the Shadow Forest are no problem for Arin in his brand-new buggy. Its four enormous wheels provide superb suspension, while the handy hooks on the back help the buggy swing and climb over rocky obstacles.

Hooks can catch enemies

Arin drives from an enclosed cockpit

SET NAME: Arin's Ninja Off-Road Buggy Car
SET NUMBER: 71811
PIECES: 267
MINIFIGURES: 4

WOW! The latest lineup of Ninja vehicles is better than ever—thanks to inventor Sora's tech genius!

SPINJITZU RACE CAR

The Dragon Hunters are no match for Zane in his awesome race car. Using dragon power to activate Spinjitzu, the vehicle can launch into a high-speed spin that sends enemies flying!

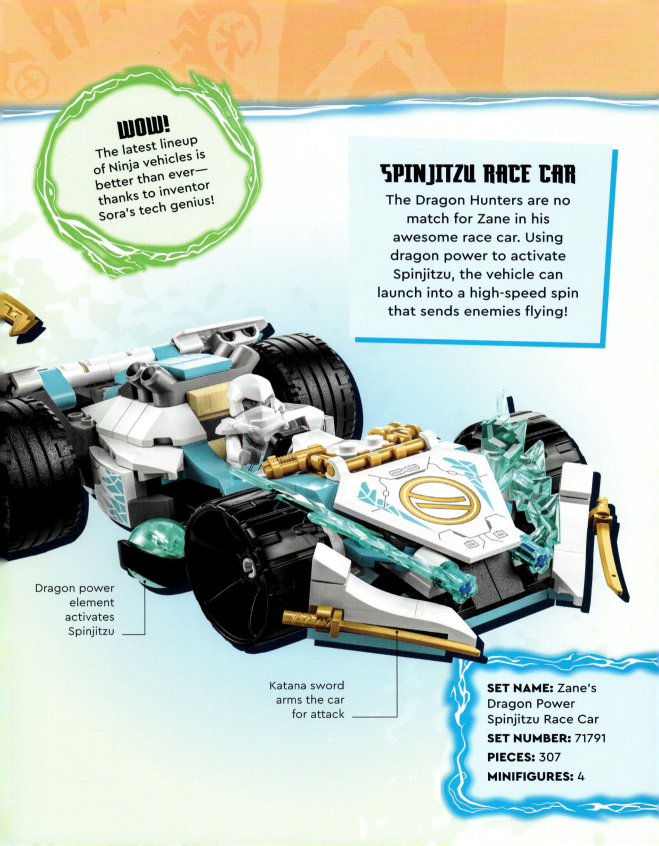

Dragon power element activates Spinjitzu

Katana sword arms the car for attack

SET NAME: Zane's Dragon Power Spinjitzu Race Car
SET NUMBER: 71791
PIECES: 307
MINIFIGURES: 4

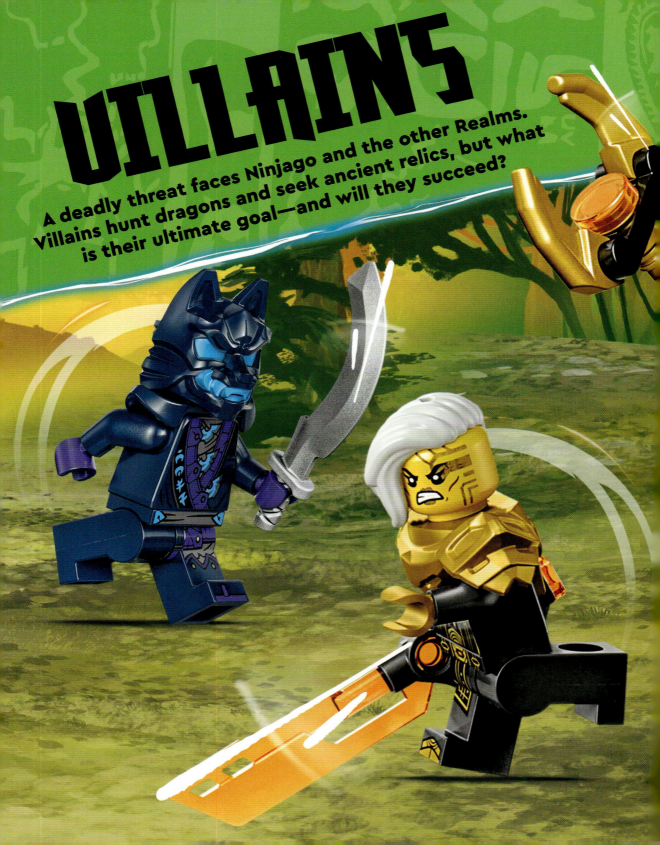

VILLAINS

A deadly threat faces Ninjago and the other Realms. Villains hunt dragons and seek ancient relics, but what is their ultimate goal—and will they succeed?

EMPRESS BEATRIX
RULER OF IMPERIUM

Empress Beatrix takes energy from dragons, by force. Dragon power has given strength to her army and helped her shape Imperium into a rule-following society. Now she plots to do the same across the other Realms.

— Imperium markings

— Grand robes of Imperium

FACT FILE
Known for: Strong leadership
Likes: Perfection
Dislikes: Failure
Watch out for: Her cruelty to dragons

WOW!
Beatrix's full title is Empress Beatrix Vaspasian-Orus, Absolute Ruler of Imperium and Protector of the True Path. What a mouthful!

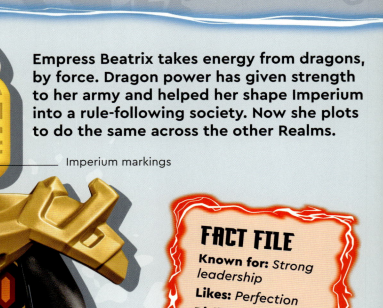

BIG SECRET
Beatrix was known as "The Good Empress" to the people of Imperium—until they found out that draining the energy from dragons harms them.

LORD RAS ARMY LEADER

With the face of a tiger and a fierce temper to match, Lord Ras expects nothing less than perfection from his underlings. If anyone messes up, they fear his anger!

Pink tiger stripes

BOSSY BOSS
Ras fiercely commands the Claw army. He's so bad-tempered, he even barks orders at Dr. LaRow!

Golden cuffs with Imperium insignia

Extravagant red robes

FACT FILE
Known for: Ferocious temper
Likes: Victory
Dislikes: Being called "That weird tiger guy"
Watch out for: His powerful hammer

WOW!
In his attempt to rule over the kingdoms, Ras seeks to unlock dark powers from ancient Elemental Masters!

IMPERIUM GUARD OBEDIENT ENFORCER

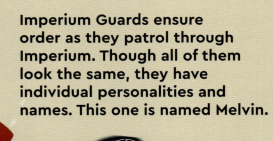

Imperium Guards ensure order as they patrol through Imperium. Though all of them look the same, they have individual personalities and names. This one is named Melvin.

Metal shoulder pads polished daily!

FACT FILE
Known for: Scratch-free armor
Likes: Shoulder pads
Dislikes: Rule breakers
Watch out for: Severe lack of humor

WOW!
Imperium has some strange rules—like insisting Guards wear shoulder pads on weekdays!

Armor glows with dragon energy

YOU MAY PROCEED
An Imperium Guard checked the Ninja's ID badges at the security station. He chooses not to question Arin's strange undercover name—Dr. Lampshade Floortile!

IMPERIUM GUARD COMMANDER SECURITY BOSS

Tasked with Imperium security, Guard Commanders oversee their troops daily. They are good at following orders, and making sure others obey them. But they are useless at thinking for themselves.

LAW AND ORDER

Thanks to the strict patrol of the Imperium Guard, crime is almost nonexistent in Imperium. Sadly, dragon-power draining is not against the law.

FACT FILE
Known for: *Being bossy*
Likes: *Giving orders*
Dislikes: *Disorder*
Watch out for: *A tendency to give very boring speeches*

Protective thigh plates

Reinforced boots make a loud stomping sound!

WOW!
Everything in Imperium is powered by dragon energy. That includes the armor of its guards and soldiers!

DRAGON HUNTER HOUND

Imperium's Dragon Hunters ride into battle on enormous hounds. But these aren't living creatures, they are Photacs—digital beasts made of hard light. Photacs pose a serious problem for the Ninja because they can deflect Elemental Energy. Uh-oh!

Glowing orange eye scares enemies

PHOTAC ARMY

Photacs are unleashed from a high-tech ball device. They are solid, powerful, and unfortunately for the Ninja, impossible to destroy!

WOW!
Photacs were invented by Sora, as cute digital pets. But Dr. LaRow turned them into fearsome monsters!

Impressive claws for attacking dragons

PHOTAC BEAST

SET NAME: Imperium Dragon Hunter Hound
SET NUMBER: 71790
PIECES: 198
MINIFIGURES: 3

Missile launchers can be set up on back

SORA'S CHALLENGE

Photacs might be indestructible, but that doesn't mean you should give up. What can you build or launch to slow the Photacs down if they attack?

Saddle for an Imperium Claw General

Imperium colors make it clear whose side the Photac is on

IMPERIUM CLAW HUNTER SOLDIER OF THE IMPERIUM

Helmet resembles dragon horns

Gleaming golden armor is surprisingly heavy to wear!

The Claw Hunters of Imperium are treated like celebrities in the city. It's possible their fame has distracted them from their training, though, as they often come out on the losing side of a battle!

FACT FILE
Known for: Mask with two sets of eyes
Likes: Birthdays
Dislikes: Stinging techno-bees
Watch out for: Dragon-powered weapon

WOW!
Claw Hunters use drones from their hover chariots to chain and carry dragons back to their own Realm.

UNDERGROUND TUNNELS
The Claw Hunters take dragons and other prisoners through the tunnels beneath Imperium. But when Riyu, Arin, and Sora were captured, Lloyd managed to find and free them!

IMPERIUM CLAW GENERAL ACE DRAGON HUNTER

The Claw Generals pride themselves on being the best of the best—and they make sure everyone knows it! These elite Dragon Hunters are trained for the most secretive and dangerous missions.

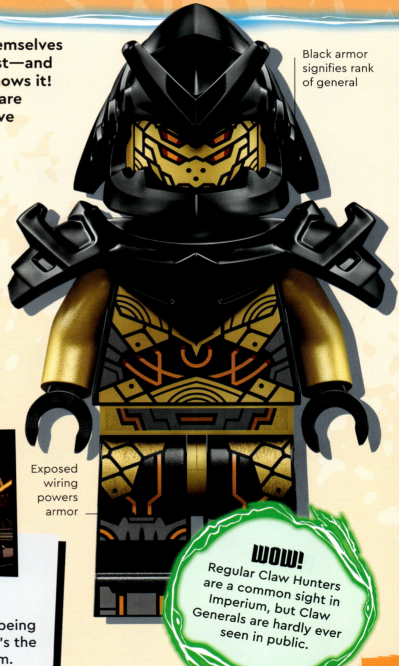

Black armor signifies rank of general

Exposed wiring powers armor

FACT FILE
Known for: Fierce leadership style
Likes: Danger
Dislikes: Weakness in others
Watch out for: Severe arrogance

RISING IN RANK
Most Claw Hunters dream of being promoted to Claw General. It's the ultimate praise in Imperium.

WOW!
Regular Claw Hunters are a common sight in Imperium, but Claw Generals are hardly ever seen in public.

RAPTON DRAGON BOUNTY HUNTER

Red visor makes it hard to read his mood

Rapton once led the Imperium Claw Hunters to capture dragons for Empress Beatrix. He thinks he's the best Dragon Hunter, but overconfidence often leads to silly mistakes!

STEALTH CAPTURE

Rapton used the chaos of MergeQuakes to capture dragons. While everyone was busy, he and his Claws snuck in and took them!

WOW! Rapton's favorite hobby is collecting delicate unicorn figurines!

Armor infused with dragon energy

FACT FILE

Known for: His evil laugh

Likes: Fighting

Dislikes: Being mocked

Watch out for: His hover chariot with detachable drones

JORDANA SORA'S NEMESIS

Jordana used to research dragons with Imperium's top scientist, Dr. LaRow. She is so jealous of Sora that she considers her a lifelong rival. But Sora can barely remember who Jordana is!

FACT FILE

Known for: *Always being second best*

Likes: *Praise. Especially from Dr. LaRow*

Dislikes: *Not being remembered*

Watch out for: *Her long-held grudges*

Markings similar to those of Dr. LaRow

Wolf Mask Army robes

RIVAL'S REVENGE

Jordana devotes her life to achieving more than Sora. She is desperate to ensure Sora never forgets her again. But she was no match for Sora and Arin's attack!

WOW! After being beaten by Sora (again!) Jordana lost faith in her research. She followed a darker path and joined Lord Ras's Wolf Mask Army.

CINDER MASTER OF SMOKE

Arriving in a puff of smoke, this Elemental Master's powers are shrouded in mystery. When Cinder unleashed an extraordinary new fighting technique called Shatterspin, the Ninja were totally shocked.

Armor like billowing smoke

SHATTERING STRENGTH

At the request of Lord Ras, Cinder steals the Mallet of Shattering. Can this ancient relic really make him unstoppable?

Wolf emblem shows allegiance to Ras

WOW!
Before the Ninja found out his true identity, Cinder was thought to be a thief called "Night Ghost."

FACT FILE
Known for: Rarely opening doors!
Likes: Provoking the Ninja
Dislikes: Jordana getting attention
Watch out for: His powerful Shatterspin

WOLF MASK WARRIOR FEARSOME SOLDIER

The Wolf Mask Army fights for an evil master. By wearing a Wolf Mask that was stolen from a sacred temple, they can gain access to immense strength—but will also lose all inner goodness.

Eyes glow blue in battle

FACT FILE
Known for: Fighting in large packs
Likes: Growling
Dislikes: Fighting without claws
Watch out for: A rising Blood Moon

Chain of claws

BEASTLY BLADES
Once a Wolf Mask's unimaginable strength has been activated, the warriors lash at opponents using their scarily sharp claw blades.

WOW!
The Wolf Army first appears in Lloyd's nightmarish visions—a forewarning of the chaos that is about to be unleashed!

43

WOLF MASK SHADOW DOJO

Deep in the Shadow Forest, Lord Ras trains his Wolf Mask Army. The dojo is fully equipped with a weapons store, training obstacles, and a battle arena. It is also home to a precious relic—and the source of Ras's power!

Intimidating architecture

Dark trees and vines surround dojo

BATTLE ARENA
Lloyd battles Cinder at the Shadow Dojo arena. The powerful Gong of Shattering is within reach, but he'll have to defeat Cinder to get it!

SET NAME: Wolf Mask Shadow Dojo
SET NUMBER: 71813
PIECES: 1,190
MINIFIGURES: 8

DRAGONS

Hunted and drained of their energy, dragons are in great danger. Together with the Ninja, they want to use their Elemental Power only for good.

SOURCE DRAGON

Source Dragons are the origin of all dragon energy. They are more powerful than anything the Ninja have ever encountered. The villains want to capture Source Dragons to harness their energy. But the brave Ninja will fight to free them at all costs!

WOW!
Source Dragons and Elemental Masters can forge a special bond. Energy flows between them, giving strength or a surge of power.

DRAGON RESCUE
Kai won't be trapped in the vines of the Shadow Forest for long. Wyldfyre will swoop to the rescue, riding Kai's fire-breathing Source Dragon!

SET NAME: Kai's Source Dragon
SET NUMBER: 71815
PIECES: 120
MINIFIGURES: 4

Flaming wings burn with dragon energy

POWER SOURCE
The Ninja had no idea that Source Dragons existed until they found one imprisoned beneath Imperium!

Sharp fangs as big as a person's hand!

Claws can slice through metal

49

EGALT MASTER DRAGON

Most dragons live and fly in the open, but some prefer to remain in hiding. Master Dragons are also rarely seen, although Lloyd leads his team to Egalt, a Master Dragon whose ancient wisdom might just help the Ninja save the world.

SORA'S CHALLENGE

With his "hat" and moustache, Egalt has the look of a Master! Think about the cool LEGO® elements that you have, and build a dragon in your own unique style.

Spikes have grown sharper over time

WOW!

Egalt lives alongside another Master Dragon, named Rontu. These two wise friends are also very talented Spinjitzu Masters.

Wispy dragon beard

SET NAME: Egalt the Master Dragon
SET NUMBER: 71809
PIECES: 532
MINIFIGURES: 5

EGALT'S WISDOM

When the Ninja are struggling to overcome the evil Shatterspin technique, they turn to Egalt. They hope he can teach them the fabled power of Rising Dragon.

Ragged wings show Egalt's age

Red sash gives Egalt a wise, dignified appearance

Tail blade for defense

HEATWAVE LAVA DRAGON

Heatwave, a Lava Dragon from the Wyldness, is fiercely loyal to Wyldfyre. Now part of Team Ninja, Heatwave joins them on their missions. His sharp claws and teeth make him truly formidable in battle. He will do anything to stop the Claws from capturing him again.

Kai rides Heatwave on a special saddle

WOW! Heatwave likes to drink lava. But his personality is calm and kind rather than fiery.

TRAINING WYLDFYRE

Raising Wyldfyre was no easy task—the wild child made a habit of falling out of trees! But when Wyldfyre discovered her Elemental Power, Heatwave was on hand to help her practise.

SET NAME: Heatwave Transforming Lava Dragon
SET NUMBER: 71793
PIECES: 479
MINIFIGURES: 5

Gold-covered horns have a graceful curve

Dragon power element for attack

HOVERCRAFT CHASE

Lord Ras often joins the hunt to capture dragons. His hovercraft is equipped with everything he needs: shooters, dragon-catching drones, and sharp claws. Will Heatwave be able to avoid capture?

JIRO ELEMENTAL DRAGON

Jiro was held captive in the cells of Imperium, until the Ninja freed him. Once safe in their Monastery stables, Sora gave the Elemental Dragon an upgrade. This made Jiro even more powerful, and ready to fight back against the full might of Empress Beatrix!

Armored saddle

Dragon blade is part of the upgraded wings

WOW!
Jiro is a Lightning Dragon, so he forms a special connection with Jay, the Master of Lightning. That's once Jay remembers who he is, of course!

SET NAME: Elemental Dragon vs. The Empress Mech
SET NUMBER: 71796
PIECES: 1,038
MINIFIGURES: 6

Shooters can launch weapons mid-flight

DRAGON ESCAPE

Jiro escaped from captivity along with many other dragons. They fought bravely against the Imperium Claws and the Photac beasts. Afterwards they escaped through an energy portal.

DRAGON VERSUS MECH

Upgraded Jiro can face the weapons of Imperium, but is he strong enough to defeat Empress Beatrix herself? The Empress battles in a golden mech with a spinning claw. Jiro, look out!

RIYU YOUNG DRAGON

When he first met Arin and Sora, Riyu was just a baby. Now, he's growing up fast and building a strong connection with his new friends. Riyu loves being part of Team Ninja!

WOW! Riyu's bond with Sora somehow helps her tap into her Elemental Power. Neither Riyu nor Sora fully understand it yet.

Arin is learning to ride Riyu

SET NAME: Young Dragon Riyu
SET NUMBER: 71810
PIECES: 132
MINIFIGURES: 3

Wings have grown large enough for flight

Determined expression

DRAGON CLAN
Riyu's clan comes from the Land of the Three Mountains. But the friendly young dragon chooses to stay with Arin and Sora instead of going back home.

RISING DRAGON
A TRICKY TECHNIQUE

Learning a new skill takes a lot of hard work, and the rare Rising Dragon fighting style is no exception. When the Ninja finally master it, they can't wait to put it to good use.

SET NAME: Kai's Rising Dragon Strike
SET NUMBER: 71801
PIECES: 24
MINIFIGURES: 2

Jagged flame design

TRAIN YOUR BODY
After perfecting the Rising Dragon moves, Kai brings even more heat into battle with his Rising Dragon Strike!

TRAIN YOUR MIND
Nya really hates getting things wrong, but she perseveres, even though Rising Dragon is hard!

SET NAME: Nya's Rising Dragon Strike
SET NUMBER: 71802
PIECES: 26
MINIFIGURES: 2

Icy wing tips

DRAGON STONE SHRINE

The remote Dragon Stone Shrine is home to many of the things Master Wu values: the beauty of nature, a training arena, dragon imagery, plenty of books, and his favorite tea set. No wonder it's where Wu chooses to hang out!

WOW!
According to legend, the Dragon Stone Shrine is the site of a long-lost book about dragon lore.

Training grounds

Wu's favorite meditation spot

PLACE OF HISTORY
The shrine's library contains some of the oldest books in existence. Wu researches the Merge, drawing on the shrine's history to help him answer his deepest questions.

SET NAME: Dragon Stone Shrine
SET NUMBER: 71819
PIECES: 1,212
MINIFIGURES: 6

Stone shaped like a dragon

Calming waterfall

Ancient tree roots

GLOSSARY

ADMINISTRATION
A bureaucratic city where nothing ever seems to get done.

CLAWS
Dragon Hunters from the kingdom of Imperium.

CLOUD KINGDOM
A peaceful Realm, inhabited by monks known as the Writers of Destiny.

CRAGLINGS
Rock creatures that live in the Kingdom of Madness.

CROSSROADS
A neighborhood that sprang up at the epicenter of the Merge. People from all Realms live there.

DOJO
A training ground specifically designed for martial arts practice.

DRAGON ENERGY CORES
A set of three mystical items that hold the power to stop MergeQuakes.

ELEMENTAL MASTER
An individual who wields a specific Elemental Power.

ELEMENTAL POWER
A power (originating from Source Dragons) that harnesses an element, such as fire or water.

GONG OF SHATTERING
A relic that can shatter the inner goodness of anyone wearing a Wolf Mask. It also allows Elemental Masters to perform Shatterspin.

IMPERIUM
A dazzling, high-tech kingdom that draws its power from dragon energy.

KINGDOM OF MADNESS
A dark Realm inhabited by mud creatures and Craglings.

LAND OF LOST THINGS
A Realm that attracts the lost people and objects of other Realms.

MECH
A large, mobile suit of mechanized armor.

MERGE
A chaotic event that disrupted the world, leaving people missing or displaced. It resulted in all known Realms appearing and existing side by side.

MERGEQUAKES
Aftershocks of the Merge, in which Realms become unstable or open up within other Realms.

NINDROID
Half ninja, half android.

REALM
World or kingdom.

RISING DRAGON
The only martial arts technique that can beat Shatterspin.

SHADOW FOREST
A dark forest where Lord Ras and his army have built a base.

SHATTERSPIN
A fierce fighting technique used by Elemental Masters who have been empowered by the Gong of Shattering.

SOURCE DRAGON
An enormous dragon of unthinkable power.

SPINJITZU
A martial arts technique where the user spins rapidly, creating a fast and forceful tornado of energy around them.

UNITED REALMS
The collective name for all of the Realms that coexist since the Merge.

WORLD FOREST
An ancient forest that contains the Temple of the Dragon Energy Cores.

WYLDNESS
A Realm of fire and lava.

INDEX

Main entries are in **bold**

A
Administration 23
Agent Walker 23
Arin **8**, 9, 14, 20, 21, 28, 34, 41, 56

B
Blazey H. Speed 19

C
Chamille 18
Cinder **42**, 44
Cloud Kingdom 22
Cole **25**
Craglings 22
Crossroads 8, 9
Crossroads citizens **18–19**
Crossroads markets **16–17**
Cyrus Borg 19

D
Destiny's Bounty 12, **14–15**
Dragon Energy Cores 11, 26, 27
Dragon Hunter Hound **36–37**
Dragon Hunters 19, 29, 36–37, 39, 40
Dragon Stone Shrine **58–59**
Dr. LaRow 9, 33, 36, 41

E
Egalt **50–51**
Elemental Dragon **54–55**
Elemental Fire Mech 21
Elemental Masters 12, 18, 22, 42, 48
Elemental Powers 9, 28, 52
Empress Beatrix 5, 20, 26, **32**, 33, 54, 55

G
Gayle Gossip 17, 19
Gong of Shattering 44, 45
Green Ninja 8, 10, **11**

H
Heatwave 13, **52–53**
Hounddog McBrag 18

I
Imperium 5, 9, 13, 24, 32–41, 49, 54, 55
Imperium Claw General 37, **39**
Imperium Guard **34**, 35

J
Jay **23**, 54
Jiro **54–55**
Jordana **41**, 42

K
Kai **12**, 13, 21, 24, 48, 52, 57

L
Land of Lost Things 25
Land of the Three Mountains 56
Lava Dragon **52–53**
Lloyd 8, 10, **11**, 14, 20, 21, 24, 26, 38, 43, 44, 50
Lord Ras 5, **33**, 41, 42, 44, 53

M
Master Dragon **50–51**
Master Wu **10**, 11, 58
Mech Bike Racer 20
Mechs 5, **20–21**, 55
Merge 10, 12, 15, 16, 19, 22, 23, 24, 25, 58
MergeQuakes 11, 12, 40
Monastery of Spinjitzu 12

N
Nindroid 24
Ninja Team Mechs 21
Nya **22**, 24, 57

O
Off-Road Buggy Car 28

P
Photacs **36–37**
Prime Empire 19

R
Rapton **40**
Realms 10, 11, 12, 14, 16, 18, 19, 30, 32
Rising Dragon 51, **57**
Riyu 9, 38, **56**
Rookery 25

S
Shadow Forest 28, 44, 48
Shatterspin 42, 45, 51
Sora 8, **9**, 14, 17, 20, 22, 26, 29, 36, 37, 38, 41, 50, 54, 56
Source Dragon **48–49**
Spinjitzu 8, 12, 29, 50
Spirit of the Temple **26–27**

T
Temple of the Dragon Energy Cores **26–27**
Tournament of Elements 18

U
United Realms 11, 14

V
Vehicles 5, 9, **28–29**

W
Wolf Mask Army 41, **43**, 44
Wolf Mask Shadow Dojo **44–45**
World Forest 26
Wyldfyre **13**, 48, 52
Wyldness 13, 52

Z
Zane **24**, 29

Project Editor Lara Hutcheson
Designers Thelma-Jane Robb, Isabelle Merry
Senior Production Editor Jennifer Murray
Senior Production Controller Lloyd Robertson
Managing Editor Paula Regan
Managing Art Editor Jo Connor
Managing Director Mark Searle
Written by Shari Last

DK would like to thank: Randi K. Sørensen, Heidi K. Jensen, Martin Leighton Lindhardt, Christina Burcea, Dimitrios Stamatis, and Tommy Kalmar at the LEGO Group; Selina Wood for proofreading and Gary Ombler for additional photography.

First American Edition, 2024
Published in the United States by DK Publishing,
a division of Penguin Random House LLC
1745 Broadway, 20th Floor, New York, NY 10019

Page design copyright © 2024 Dorling Kindersley Limited
www.LEGO.com/ninjago

24 25 26 27 28 10 9 8 7 6 5 4 3 2 1
001–341655–July/2024

LEGO, the LEGO logo, the Minifigure, the Brick and Knob configurations, NINJAGO, and the NINJAGO logo are trademarks and/or copyrights of the LEGO Group. ©2024 The LEGO Group.

Manufactured by Dorling Kindersley,
One Embassy Gardens, 8 Viaduct Gardens, London SW11 7BW
under license from the LEGO Group.

All rights reserved.
Without limiting the rights under the copyright reserved above, no part of this publication may be reproduced, stored in or introduced into a retrieval system, or transmitted, in any form, or by any means (electronic, mechanical, photocopying, recording, or otherwise), without the prior written permission of the copyright owner.
Published in Great Britain by Dorling Kindersley Limited

A CIP catalog record for this book is available
from the Library of Congress

ISBN: 978-0-5938-4178-5 (hardcover)
ISBN: 978-0-5938-4179-2 (library edition)

Printed and bound in China

www.dk.com
www.LEGO.com

This book was made with Forest Stewardship Council™ certified paper – one small step in DK's commitment to a sustainable future. Learn more at www.dk.com/uk/information/sustainability

Your opinion matters

Please scan this QR code to give feedback to help us enhance your future experiences